Whole Heart for Girls
Feeling Good About Yourself

Amy L. Stark, Ph.D.

DEDICATION

I dedicate this book to my mother, Irene.
The woman who always loved me and cared if I loved myself.

CONTENTS

ACKNOWLEDGMENTS

I want to thank all the children and teens I have worked with over the years. Through them, I have learned so much about where self-esteem issues start and the importance of addressing them early on. They have also taught me that self esteem is a journey not a destination. I also wish to thank my editor, Lisa Houser, for her guidance and assistance.

1

DESERVING OF LOVE

"Give it your whole heart." That's what people say to encourage you to do your best. But what if your whole heart isn't whole? What if it has holes in it instead? In fact, what if there are holes where your feelings about you live? How can you give your "whole heart" then?

You were born and you were perfectly loveable. Not because you had all your fingers and toes, or your mother's eyes and your father's chin—but because you truly were a perfect, unique, human being. You didn't even have to DO anything to deserve love.

At that moment you deserved love just because you were you. And because you were born loveable, you can say "I am loveable" three times.

2

A HEART HOLE

You went home from the hospital and cried and ate and slept and grew. Sometimes you cried so hard that your parents couldn't calm you down. That's what babies do.

But sometimes the grown-ups grew tired or were in a hurry. Sometimes they got mad at other drivers or someone at the drive-through window. Sometimes they disagreed with each other. And while all that was happening around you, a tiny hole in the part of your heart that cares about you appeared.

3

THE HOLE GROWS

As you grew and went out into the world to discover what was there, you heard, "No!" or "That's enough of that" or "Why can't you listen to me?"

Because everyone makes mistakes, even grown-ups, you wondered if when you make a mistake if something was wrong with you. And the hole in the part of your heart that cares about you grew.

You grew bigger and went off to school and found that all the children in your class have holes, too. You knew they were there when you listened carefully to the things they said to each other. "You look like a hockey stick with hair," someone said to a skinny child. "Hey, Fatso," they shouted to an overweight girl. They even insult each others' families, "Your mother is sooooo ugly."

And you feel embarrassed and angry and hurt—as if no one likes you anymore. You must have done something wrong or the kids wouldn't be teasing you, right? You feel unlikeable, and even unlovable, sometimes.

And the hole grows.

4

SCHOOL & SPORTS

Teachers aren't all the same. Some teachers are supportive and build you up. They praise your efforts and applaud your improvements. Then the hole stays the same for a while—sometimes it even fills in a bit.

Sometimes teachers or grown-ups at the school have bad days, too. They might use a grouchy voice that hurts your feelings. When they tell you what you did wrong, you feel bad, like you can't ever seem to get anything right. And so the hole in the part of your heart that cares about you grows.

Some coaches are positive and they teach you to not give up but to practice. They notice when you try and when you improve. And the hole fills in a bit.

Other coaches scold you when you miss a shot or are not playing your best. They get angry at you and make you feel like you aren't good enough. And so the hole in the part of your heart that cares about you grows.

5

KINDNESS

All around your friends have holes growing. Life's ups and downs affect everyone.

Some become very quiet.

Some try not to make any mistakes.

Some are loud and annoying to gain negative attention instead of no attention at all.

What will you do? You must learn to fill the hole in the part of your heart that cares about you.

No matter what anyone tells you, you deserve love—just like on the day you were born.

And even if someone says you are purple with green spots, that doesn't make it true. And if someone calls you a ding dang do-do head—even if that someone is important to you, like your cousin Mike or your Great-Grandma Rose—you don't have to believe them. It can be your secret to think to yourself, "I am loveable – no matter what anyone else says."

And if someone is mean to you, that doesn't mean you deserve it. You are loveable — just the way you are. You are special enough to find friends who will treat you nicely—the way that you deserve to be treated.

So when you feel lonely and hurt and the hole in the part of your heart that cares about you feels like it is growing, remind yourself, "I am loveable."

Choose friends who are kind to you. That's how good friends treat each other. And remember that everyone else has a little hole, too. Try to be kind to them, as well. After all, everyone wants to give their whole heart—not their hole heart.

6

THE AMAZING YOU

When you hit a bump in the road—maybe you don't make the team, or your math grade isn't quite what you hoped it would be—remember that it's not the end of the road. Just a bump. There's plenty of road ahead to travel. You can practice, practice, practice for the team and study, study, study your math. You'll soon come to another opportunity to show what you can do. With your hard work, next time you'll shine.

No matter what, you're still loveable. Don't forget to tell yourself how loveable you are. The part of your heart that cares about you likes to hear it.

And since you are in charge of your happily ever after, you will live happily ever after from now on. Oh, but instead of this being the end, this is just the beginning—the beginning of a whole new you.

7

DISCUSSION QUESTIONS

1. When you are in a group of friends, how often do you check to make sure you have not left someone out? Why is that important?

We have all been left out at one time or another. It does not feel very good.

Think how nice it would have felt to you if someone would have asked you to join in and be included.

Can you think of a nice way to do that and actually try that at school?

2. If your friends make fun of someone, how can you discuss how it must feel with them? Is there a way you could reach out to the person they are picking on?

What if you said to your friends that "if someone spoke that way to them it would really hurt their feelings."

Can you talk about something else? Can you go and make sure the person they were picking on is not hurt and tell them you are sorry that happened to them?

3. If a teacher or someone at the school is mean or yells at you, who could you tell? If they do it to someone else, what should you do?

You should always try to talk to someone at the school first. Tell a grown-up you trust at the school and try to get their help.

Also tell your mom or dad so they can help you.

If a coach is mean to you at a practice, ask your mom and dad for help.

4. If someone you thought was a friend picks on other people, should you stop them? What if they start to do it to you?

Tell your friend that it makes you sad when they are mean to the other kids. If they are really a good friend maybe they can tell you why they are doing that.

If your friend does that to you, tell them they are hurting your feelings. If they don't seem to care, look around and spend time with someone else.

Maybe your friend is having a bad day. If your friend keeps doing this to you, perhaps you need a break from each other. Tell your friend you want them to be nice to you and if they can't do that, maybe you should each find other friends to be with.

8

ACTIVITIES

1. Research the meaning of your name. Why were you given that name...ask your parents. Look up the meaning of your name.

2. Ask 5 people you know what they find special about you. Record their answers

3. Write down what you love most about yourself. Leave room so that once a year you can re-enter or edit the top 5 things. Do this for three years.

Amy L. Stark, Ph.D.

ABOUT THE AUTHOR

Dr. Amy Stark, Ph.D. is a highly respected clinical psychologist in the state of California. She received her doctorate in 1981 from the California School of Professional Psychology in San Diego, and her background in education is in child psychology.

Dr. Stark is best known for her work with high-conflict divorce situations. Due to the fact that Dr. Stark's training is in child psychology, she brings that expertise in her work with children of high-conflict divorce.

One of the unique techniques that Dr. Stark brings into play while working with children is the presence of her new therapy dog Gregory. Along the years, many kids and teenagers have attested to how their therapy sessions with Dr. Stark were facilitated simply by the fact that her therapy dogs Jimmy and Rita were present there! Now that Gregory is the new therapy dog, they'll feel the same way about him.

In addition, Dr. Stark is the author of a series of illustrated children's books The Fairy Godmother Next Door and The Fairy Godmother Babysits. All of her books are available on amazon.com

For more information: www.dramystark.com

Amy L. Stark, Ph.D.

Made in United States
North Haven, CT
17 December 2023

45971885R00015